Discover Endless Possibilities

Reimagining the World

Facebook Marketing Strategies

Violet Jeanes

Why Facebook?

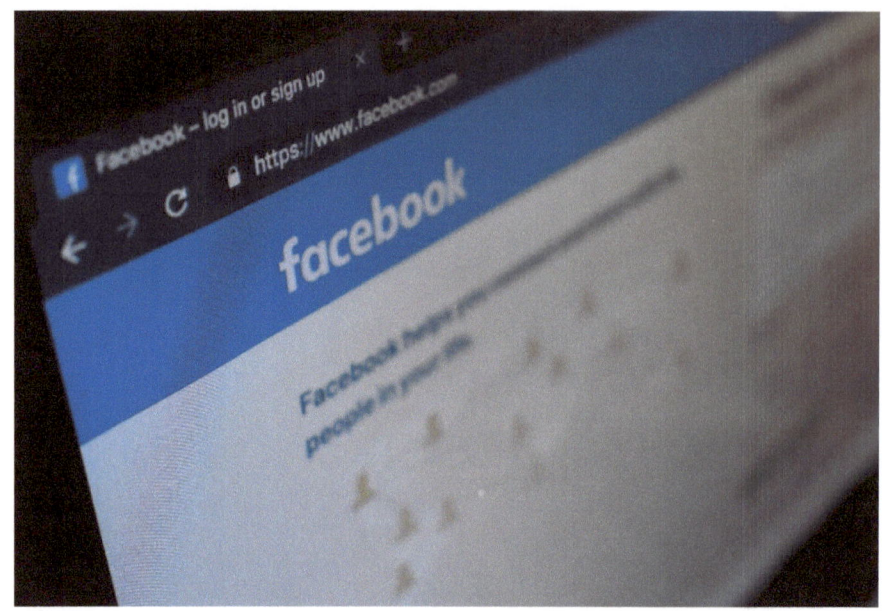

Welcome to the world of Facebook, a world so unique, genuine and full of possibilities! It is a special place uniting all populations, genders and ages. The platform initially started off as a form of online student directory that consisted of photos and basic information, and has since evolved into a universal website that would allow people from all over the world to connect with each other.

In today's modern economy, the huge amounts of competition that startups and companies face often push them to constantly evolve and diversify to stay relevant to their customers. Businesses that fail to do so will find it hard to survive in the economy, much less thrive in it. However, Facebook is a good example of a company that is able to do that.

For more than ten years, it has been one of the leading platforms for connecting people, and is constantly updating and diversifying their business, even buying the rights to Instagram and Whatsapp to ensure they constantly have a source of income.

Of course, simply being a social media platform means that there is no physical product being sold, and the business means nothing without its users. In terms of Facebook, this refers to business trying to market their products, and regular users of the service.

Marketing a product comes in 2 main forms- reaching out to customers via individuals that receive various forms of benefits from selling a product (outbound), or creating engaging content to attract individuals to buy your products (inbound).

As our world becomes more technology-oriented, more and more businesses insist on creating engaging content instead of commissioning marketing individuals to reach out to potential customers. Why is this the case?

In the case of outbound marketing, the main factor engaging customers is the people, the marketing individuals that are made to engage potential customers- but there is a limitation to how many people you can reach out to, and your potential customers are capped. Simply put, you can only attract as many people as your marketers reach out to.

The whole process goes a lot more smoothly nowadays. Businesses attract consumers by inbound, not outbound marketing- and their best marketers focus more on creating engaging content that would appeal to consumers. In this day and age, people should realize your content is valuable on their own, so they get to the content themselves (not the other way around). With everything so widely available and at such a low-level of differentiation, products need to have an edge that allows them to stand out from the crowd.

Facebook is a huge phenomenon. With over a billion monthly active users (and counting), it is a one of a kind community that has a bigger population than any country in the world. The special online Facebook community unites people from all nations, genders and ages.

The sheer size and importance of the platform makes marketing on social media platforms such as Facebook essential for businesses aiming to increase sales. But the icing on the cake is that apart from the vastness of the potential audience that the business can reach, the marketer also obtains the ability to filter through these potential customers, and cater certain products to different profiles of people that they may be targeting.

Last, but definitely not the least, all of that is accomplished with a small financial contribution (a special topic to be explained later)! A small investment in marketing is always worth it, because marketing does not provide a definite return - there is no way to project your earnings over a specified period of time.

Although some may think that this statement was contradictory with the belief that marketing is a branch worth investing a lot, the general truth is (that most marketing specialists try to avoid) that it mostly relies on the "trial-and-error" procedure. It is possible and very common in the industry to lose money in investments while earning insufficient income.

But, luckily, Facebook stepped in to improve this situation. With little to no investments attached, it allows businesses to generate substantial sales from it, and incentivises users to continue using the platform since they won't be constantly bombarded with pushy ads from companies they aren't even interested in.

With all these benefits to Facebook marketing, it's about time you'd begin to wonder: How can I then market to customers on the site? Without further ado, I'll start with my example-packed strategy guide aimed at both beginners in entrepreneurship, and to those that want to know how to evolve and improve their business.

1. Get to know the tools

Physics has Watts, Teslas, meters per second, chemistry has moles, and social media has something totally different to use for metrics. Yes, like many natural sciences, Facebook needs to have certain units of measurement for marketers to know if they're doing the right thing. In a whole ocean of metric variables to follow, I have to emphasize the most important ones.

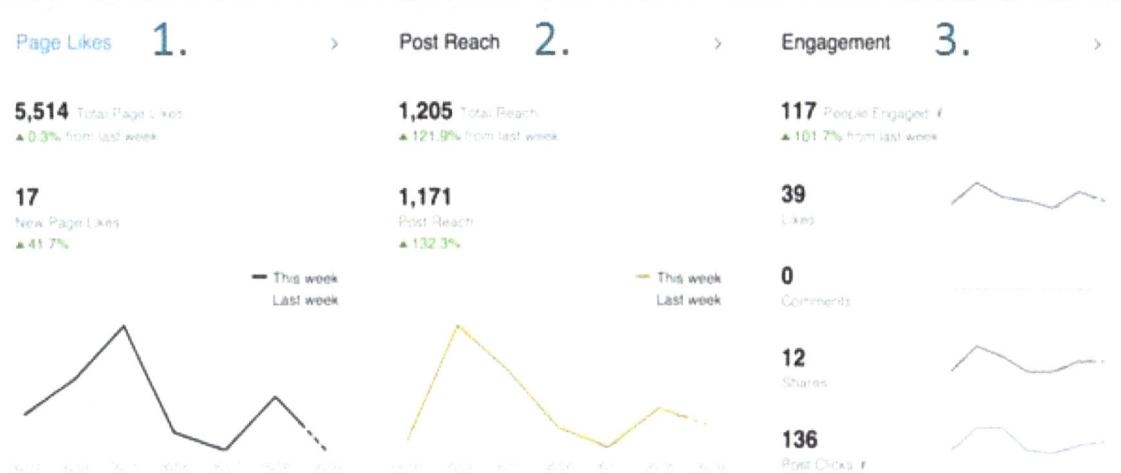

First of all, Facebook Insights has to be mentioned due to the comprehensive metrics it has to offer to potential marketers. If you possess various pages, you can manage all of them on the Platform Insights page, There you will be able to see all of the basic metrics: likes, comments, shares, reach and visits.

- Total Page Likes represent the number of new users that have liked your page in the period of the last seven days, and plots a graph that conveniently allows you to see the rise (let's hope there won't be falls) in likes compared to the previous weekly period.

- Reach is a metric that tells you the number of people who got in touch with your content specifically, by any means during the last seven days, i.e. viewing your page, liking your content, following your page..etc

3. Engagement is the number of individuals that have either clicked, liked or shared your content in a week.

The same metrics are applied to narrow it down to your last five posts or competitors' pages.

Net Likes
Net likes shows the number of new likes minus the number of unlikes.

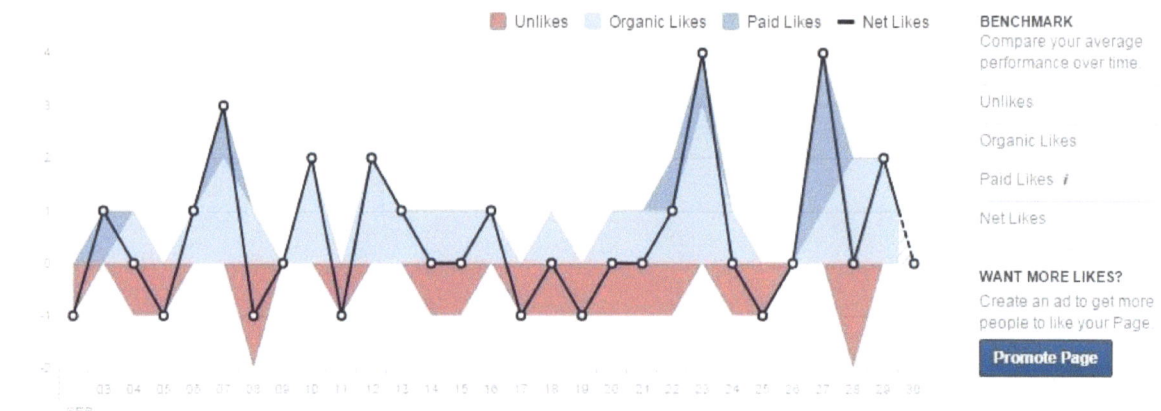

Despite the fact that I personally don't like graphs, I have to mention these are quite simple to analyse and understand. The graph above specifically represents the flow of likes and unlikes. But this is a good standpoint to make a distinction in likes. Statistically speaking, a like is a like, and it counts anyway. But in terms of generating sales, paid likes probably won't result in new faithful customers, or not much of them. The key is to gain organic likes, and like the name explains, an organic like is proof that your content genuinely interacted with someone, and isn't a one-off thing that happened simply because the ad appeared on the user's page. That's the type of likes every good marketer should be aiming at.

Where Your Page Likes Happened
The number of times your Page was liked, broken down by where it happened.

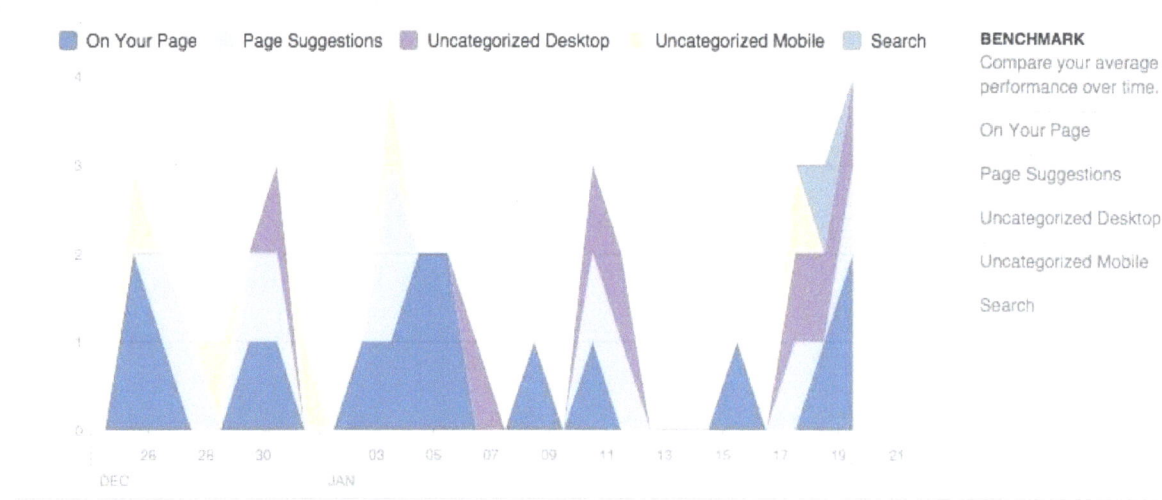

Another graph shows us the source of any kind of engagement. It is essential for directing your focus on a field of property where your content does best at. In that way, you could set a group of similar pages (consisting of competition) and follow them. causing your page to show up as a suggestion when somebody likes the competitor's page.

2. Set goals

As implied earlier, it's all about the sales. Nonetheless, if you have any kind of business selling products or services, rentability is the main principle you should follow. The more you sell, the better the financial outcome. Even if financial gain isn't your main focus, if you feel the urge that your business needs to accomplish something else (we'll discuss that later on), you need to set milestones to help you ascertain if you're going in the right way. Also, they could be the perfect motivators of self- accomplishment. Of course, within a business, organisational value is just as important as high sales; sales should not be the only defining factor of the success of your business.

In order to have a motivating goal, a goal that'll make you "go all in" and make a huge effort, it has to be SMART. S stands for Specific, M for Measurable, A for Achievable, R for Real and T for Time-related. To have a goal defined by those attributes is much more motivating than having the "I'll do my best" attitude.

Your Facebook strategy and goal shouldn't be isolated from the world, and should instead be integrated with other goals and segments of doing business. But, some general goals can be put out as doing best for most marketers:

- Boosting brand awareness – Even if you possess the ultimate, inexpensive, do-it all crème de la crème product on the marketplace, you won't be able to sell it if no one knows it exists. The truth of the matter is that some sub-par products and services get more exposure than actual higher quality ones, due to higher brand awareness. So, before you hope sales start falling from the sky, you should set a SMART goal, for example, of reaching 500 new likes in the next week. Please keep in mind that these proportions vary with many criteria. like the actual size of your entrepreneurship in the real world by the time you set up your Facebook page. Likes often correlate to the number of people that know of your brand, meaning that being popular in stores will likely result in a better-known virtual profile. Also, if you had a Facebook page, but didn't use it well for marketing, it has to take some time to build a steady base of loyal followers since the page was idle. But don't worry, with almost no investment and huge numbers showing high engagement, Facebook is the right place, no matter what your goals include.

- Have non-colliding goals – "I want it all, I want it all, I want it all, and I want it now!", says Freddie Mercury in a famous Queen song, which ties in well to the motto of most businesses. Most entrepreneurs want more money, more customers, a great brand value, and good products at the same time, but long-time businesses will tell us that meeting all these goals are almost impossible. For example, if you want high engagement rates with a huge number of likes in a short amount of time, you would have to know that most of them would have the "ghost" character, meaning that the people who liked your page do it either because they are constantly bombarded with ads, or are likes from fake profiles (which happens a lot, but you don't want that kind of engagement for your business). Or maybe, some people flood the pages with so many posts, hoping that it will result in the exponential rise of likes and shares. Some marketers know the importance of emotional content and the psychological factor of it, but still won't splurge on the content regarding special offers; The key word is balance. Moderation and balance. It is ok if many goals are present (which would aid you well as an entrepreneur) but with time, a marketing specialist should learn that gradually all of them could possibly be accomplished, and not in an instant. For example, you'll have to focus on hiring content marketing specialists to create the essential part of your competitive advantage before you start to focus on generating new leads, and after all of that, you can invest in boosting your product once people hear of it. Like all good things in life, a good strategy takes time.

3. Divide and Conquer: Segment your audience

In order to enhance the effectiveness of your targeted marketing, you should create targeted strategies for your target audience(s). In order to tailor it to them, you should exactly know the parameters of the people you're reaching: age, gender, region etc

- Locations – The basic measurement for positioning through a marketing channel. If you sell Californian burgers, considering the type of product (food for immediate consumption), you cannot market toward New Yorkers. However, this is not to say that you can only sell to local residents - some products may be catered specifically to tourists. For example, if you own a local antique store selling trademark souvenirs, the local people surely don't need that stuff. But, the tourists have to need that.
- Demographics – Ah, welcome to the plethora of potential tools for reaching the right people.

    Data mining and Facebook algorithms allow you to discover people from various demographics- for example, relationship status. Newly wedded people are your aim if you have a honeymoon travel agency etc.
- Interests – Similar to demographics, but with a broad spectrum of options. In my opinion,   this is the best metric for the entertainment industry, because it directly refers to attributes we aren't born with, and is more representative of the true interests of consumers. Music, movies, theatre, performance are all in this field. For example, concert venues may reach out to people who have an interest in operas or orchestras, and may even use that information to determine what act they should host next.

Keeping in mind the criteria your innovation meets, you're able to select your audience to cater to their interests better with this tool. Because it has all that's important for the market: it contains hints about the ideology and behaviour of humans. From which you can connect to your target audience.

And now we come to the entity which is Facebook Insights. Although it was said above that you should select your own audience based on your advertising needs, a move that would be wiser for those with a large clientele would be for them to adapt to their audience. (Generally speaking, Facebook suggests defining an audience of 10,000 accounts or more for the optimal reach).

So, what does that mean? Facebook gives you an insight into what your generated audience looks like.

Even when specified in the beginning, you never know who may end up following. You might've ended up with a larger pool of audience than you had intended to get, and you don't know what to do with the people your content isn't catered for - but you can never have enough of the audience. This is why you need a timely adaptation to your new people who joined the target group, in terms of changing the content, time when you post etc

With this tool, you can also gain insight reports on competitors, brands or interests. The trick is to make sure you possess a similar topic to offer. Facebook is 89% accurate at finding the right people.

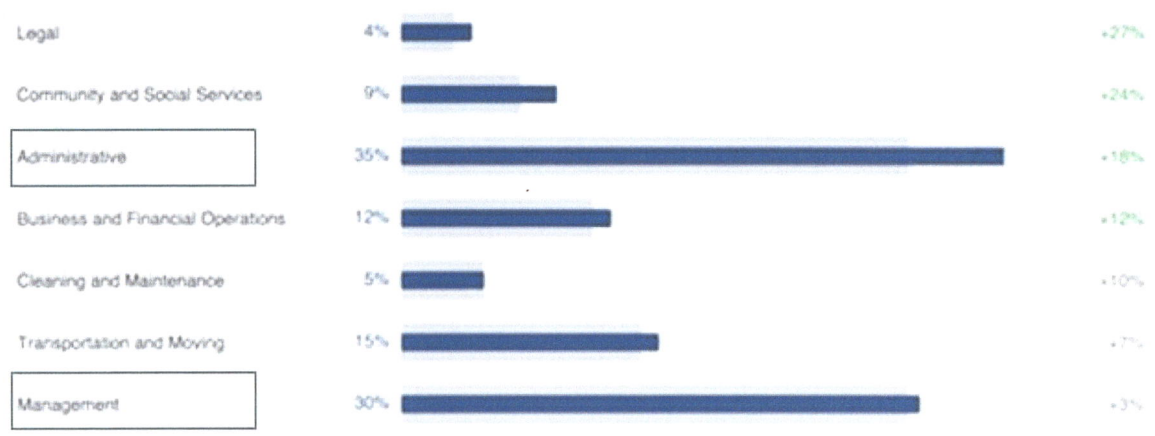

Let's have a glance at the example given above. For instance, green tea could be something you specialize in, produce and distribute. And looking at the Facebook Insight diagram, you can easily see that the majority of your audience are administrative and management specialists. Do you think that investing a little in a sponsored advertisement that has a nice visual content saying something about the health benefits of green tea in everyday consumption of hard-working managers will result in better payoff? Yes, it will!

4. Answering questions

Answering questions may be addressed 2 ways: The first way is all about respecting your customers- mainly, their needs and wishes. Research has shown that lower quality products could perform better in a battle with the higher quality ones, if the organization has customer oriented values and policies.

People nowadays often don't use call centers due to them being notorious for keeping customers on hold for long periods of time, and requires you to be available to speak. Messaging eliminates those issues and makes it much more convenient for its customers to get access to customer service.

Knowing most customers would prefer to use messaging, put yourself in your potential customers' shoes: You are interested in a television, and want to know the exact dimensions of it to ascertain if it's an appropriate size for your house. You put in a question to the shop's customer service, and they put you on hold, saying they will answer it. However, a few days have passed, but there is still no response. Another shop appears on your feed, offering a similar product for a slightly higher price. The store has five star reviews, their customer service replies with the dimensions within a day, and the store offers a 30-day refund policy for defective products. Which would you pick?

Although it seems obvious, a good Facebook marketer should have great time management when answering a customer's question. When logging in to carry out your daily page maintenance (or when training your staff to do so), you should first check to see if there are any questions pending and answer them politely. Nobody likes to be treated with disrespect, and you should treat their time as if it's your own. After all, these are the people that keep your business alive.

5. Questioning customers

Although we have just covered the essence of why you need to answer your customer's questions, it is equally as important to do the opposite. People change, and so do businesses. In order to keep in track of what your clients like and what they deem valuable, besides the regular market research which gives you some insight into their past and present interests, it is really helpful to simply ask them questions.

Your customers are your main stakeholders, and that's something a good marketer should always have in mind. Besides explaining the importance of timely responses in the previous section, gathering opinions from clients is also something that has to be done on a regular basis. Your products and services are marketed towards real people – your customers. As such, the main point is to realize that the insight you receive from a customer's feedback about an important matter is something valuable and irreplaceable. What's more, it's something that shouldn't be taken lightly. Keep in mind that many big enterprises give a huge amount of money to specialized consultant companies for providing them feedback about their way of doing business. When you realize that other companies pay people to receive information about what they're doing wrong, it is clear that Facebook brings along a new method.

You may wonder, how come? Well, by implementing questions in your day-to-day posts, asking people what they like (and what should be skipped for praising about your services), what they would like to change, and what should be continued in practice, you have for yourself a great channel of receiving valuable info for little to no money being invested. It's a pity marketers don't understand the importance of this part, as it has generally high returns much with low to nothing being invested into it.

6. Value is greater than traditional selling

More and more businesses post sales-driven content, which appear as very pushy for the typical consumer. Resourceful content provides much better value for your customers, because the main reason people go to Facebook is to relax a little and to enjoy their time. A big banner with captions like: buy, 20% sale, special offer etc. isn't a part of the great mix.

This is why you have to ensure that your content generates a context for your specific customer profile. For example, put yourself in the customer's shoes and imagine that you're the one buying the very product you sell, and think what type of content you would rather respond to:

Example 1: Click here to buy my new book for travelling newbies! My employees and I think it's really good! For only thirty bucks, it's a real money saver! Hurry up before the offer expires!

Example 2: During my long travelling experiences, I came across a lot of obstacles. Sometimes it was the money, sometimes the route, and sometimes it was finding an appropriate hotel booking. Hence, I wrote this guide to help all those vacation-hungry people to make the best travelling plan possible as I was once in the same position.

As mentioned earlier, the main point of doing up your advertisements like so is to assure customers that they will have their needs satisfied by buying your product or service instead of broadcasting out loud what's in it for you. You should employ more of a "Please tell us what you think about our services" as compared to a "30%

percent off until Thursday!". This evokes the feeling in the customer that their feedback is actually being taken seriously and they would thus be more willing to do business with you again. Facebook has changed a lot, and promotions are given less ad space in the News Feed of the customer with a ratio of about 1:10. Customers themselves admit that they don't like seeing lots of ads on their web pages so do take note, no matter what kind of marketing you're doing the customer always comes first.

7. Boost wisely

A recurring problem you might face is when you reach a limited number of potential customers despite the great content. Of course, boosting posts may seem like a great option, but the problem with financing it still persists. One should only boost your posts if they're some kind of a tycoon who is able to invest in every single post they generate, but then again, how many marketing start-ups have tons of money at their disposal? The answer? None. That's why "wisdom" is the key to this strategy. We don't possess unlimited resources to minimize failure and thus, we must choose WHERE to invest, and more specifically, WHICH post we should boost to maximize profits.

It is expected to see a big return on your investments for every dollar you spend. It won't be easy in the beginning, but with more and more practice, you could tip the odds in your favour.

Choose wisely and make sure you are strategic when managing your posts because the true art of advertising is all about being open-minded, concise and the ability to think outside of the box.

To be specific, it is unlikely that you should boost the generic and everyday posts with links to your sales page as it is close to impossible to gain a competitive advantage that way. It is always best to boost the personalized posts which appeal the most to your audience. For example, if you run a cocktail bar that has special offers for more shots ordered, skip the classic style of promoting which consists of simply taking good photos of the cheap cocktails. Instead, give value to your content by placing it in an environment full of friends chit-chatting, with a warm atmosphere filling the room. The key here is to reel the customers in by speaking directly to their heart and soul by helping them imagine a scenario in which they are a part of. This evokes a sense of belonging in them and would make them more likely to want to go there and experience it themselves.

8. Affiliated brands

Your customers want to feel special. Of course they'll gain some kind of benefit by using your product, but as users of your particular product or service, they want to be different from the crowd. This is where the business intelligence of the entrepreneur comes in. Be picky when it comes to corporate partnerships and special access. Customers always have that in mind when shopping and choosing what's right for them.

For example, one such example could be that you sell fashionable artisanal shoes made from leather. They are hard to clean and keep in good shape, they are hand- made and prone to scratches making them hard to maintain. The customer than probably thinks: "Hey, I've paid a lot for this pair of black suede loafers, but I don't see how can I keep them clean all the time?". This is when you have to start thinking about corporate strategies in terms of good marketing practice. Find appropriate leather care companies and create special offers for a packet of complementary products. That's the true value customers appreciate. By doing this, they know you're thinking about them and their needs and not just selling your product for profit.

This way, customers get to know other brands which are essential for your services, as well as feeling unique due to the special access to offers, package giveaways etc… It is also good for general business sustainability as you get to level up other enterprises (who make your "business friends" in terms of what they sell, not competitive enemies) and to make cross-promotions with them.

9.   Posting frequency

I always know when McDonalds delivers a new burger. I'm always aware of that because I see the advertisements for them so many times on television and on billboards, so much so that I have it almost visualized perfectly in my head every time I think of it. With this in mind, how much content should we use to hook customers in?

We want to attract our customers with enough material, but not too much to the point that we drive them away every time we post something. But then again, the term "enough" represents a different amount of posts for each particular business. The key point is to give the audience the wanted and needed information and content without being too boring. This is the part where posting needs to be lively, like a real conversation. Every good marketer should be able to tell when their imaginary interviewee gets bored. This boredom in social media is often indicated with less general engagement, and in extreme cases, negative public comments.

With that being said, statistics show that the optimal posting frequency on Facebook is about 2-3 times a day. However, each business is unique and this can lead to the numbers and sales results varying between businesses

10. Timing makes perfection

What is the point of posting at odd hours such as 3 in the morning? They're all probably
asleep, and by the time they see your post in the morning it'll be vintage to them. You need to understand the short life cycle of a post; think of it as a fast dying particle in physics. A post reaches nearly 80% of the whole audience in the first five hours of the original posting, and we can say it's a one-time-shot. This is precisely why you need to know the behavior of your target audience, and to ask yourself a few questions. When are my customers the most active? What is the local time for most of my customers? If I post on other social media platforms, do I need to instantly post on Facebook?

Here I have a special need to put focus on the non-general aspect of timely posting. It is not the same for every business, nor can it be classified by a segment of doing business. Think of it as kind of a "trial and error" procedure. Practice makes perfect. For example, if you put yourself in an unbiased, objective state of mind, and realize you have a great post but see little engagement, you can surely blame the time. After that try to share a post with similar content at a different time and observe for a certain pattern. If the second post gets more engagement, use that timetable as sort of a guideline as to when you get good engagement. Sometimes it even happens that the so called "not-so-good" posts generate sales and engagement by just being posted in the right time at the right place (which is Facebook).

11. Minimize text on pictures

A picture speaks a thousand words, and that fact too is widely applicable in Facebook marketing. People are visual creatures and media such as photos and videos have a huge impact on them. Besides that, humans tend to be very lazy when it comes to reading, so every marketer should know how to make use of this. Potential customers are always on the run, and even if they wanted to, more often than not they do not have the time to sit and read your three paragraphs of product praising text.

Design new and interesting pictures! Think of each and every one of your customers glancing at their smartphones as your "stage time" and as your opportunity to show off your product or service through your marketing skills. Create compelling pictures, photographs and memes. Make them think twice while looking at it but most importantly, know your measures. Do not simply take plain product pictures, but rather treat content as art created for showcasing your brand identity and what your business stands for. Last but not least, follow the "Less than 20% text rule" when designing pics. Sometimes, Facebook even forbids the posting of photos with more text on them.

12. Create contests and giveaways

Let's be honest, humans are competitive by nature. And when it comes to a bonus of receiving something for free, you get the essence of why consumers love contests. This is a great tool especially for beginners, and for those times during the launch of a new product when good reviews and feedback are always more than welcome.

Dedicate a day in a week for free giveaways, and generate winners through a random number generator such as random.org. Make them comment, share and like, and by doing sot, you make your product or service appear in their friend's News Feed. The point of this method is to become viral, but in a good way.

Another tip could be a task for potential contest winners to do, such as tagging their friends in the comments section below the post to directly tell them to look at your content, and maybe generate new followers. When the giveaway winner receives the product, ask him politely to write an honest opinion on your page. Note that most of the time, the opinions would be positive if the whole contest process was a good experience for them, so do make sure the delivery package is nice, and maybe add some samples for them to enjoy (cosmetics, for example).

13. The power of Word-of-mouth

Facebook plays an important part in the implementation of word-to-mouth marketing but what exactly is it all about? Well, it is essentially a type of marketing practice that is done in order to organically gain new customers through old ones. The seasoned customers tell their friends that your product is great and what's most important, is that they do that voluntarily, and not through some forced sharing strategy. Who would you rather believe the most? An internet platform telling you to buy stuff, or a sincere friend talking about authentic experiences with a particular product or service. So if you want word-to-mouth to play an important role in your strategy, Facebook management is a must. By creating a page that is widely present in social media, you make it easy for friends to refer to your business:

Situation 1

Person A: Did you taste that awesome pastry in the bakery two blocks from here? It's
absolutely delicious!

Person B: Not really. I haven't walked down that street for a month.

Situation 2:

Person A: Last night I tried so many great types of craft beer in a new pub. Those flavours were amazing!

Person B: Oh, the new Irish pub next to the museum? I've seen that a couple of my Facebook friends liked a few of their posts, it keeps appearing in my News Feed. I have to admit they have really good blends!

14. Use pics instead of articles

People mostly ignore linked articles through which so many pages post. They often think of it as annoying to transfer from the coziness of Facebook to another third-party site. However, leading customers to your website, or the affiliate's website, is usually required for good business practice. To make the whole process more appealing to people, avoid just linking the article on your website (those posts are indicated with an automatically generated post with a small thumbnail and a few sentences of text).

Instead, try posting an influential picture from your article like its own individual post, not a link, and put an interesting caption above, with the hyperlink to the website URL. This method is proven by research to draw more attention.

15.   Be visually original

Remember, authenticity matters. No matter how much better the rich, beautiful stock photos are, homemade photos are always better. People want genuine, not generic things. Your own images often tell a special story which stock photos don't carry with them, despite them being and looking more professional.

It sounds like art and science, does it? Well, the truth is that in practice, it is usually a perfect blend of your own graphics, catchy sounding titles, and quite literally simple Google images. The hard thing is learning how to mix that perfect blend, and that's the true science behind content marketing.

Customers like seeing people try everything to make content appealing, but not when they try too much. Minimalism is now trending, A good atmospherically shot carrying a special message with a few words are getting straight to the customers, and thus promoting sales.

16.   Timely cover photos

Their purpose is to reflect a certain time of the year for a business. Use them wisely. Changing them frequently enough is telling the audience you are a social media savvy entrepreneur, who is constantly involved in constantly updating their business and coming up with new campaigns.

Got a seasonal promotion for your products? Nothing is more appropriate for that than a new cover. Every time you gain a new visitor to your home page, he or she will immediately be up to date with the latest promotion, and existing customers are excited to see what new promotions are coming up.

17. Tagging as a benefit

Widen your exposure with tagging. It is cool to name the affiliates and key enterprises that help you run business, so why not take it a step further by tagging as well? Partnering with well-known brands and tagging them will allow customers of that business to discover yours more easily, since customers often look into affiliated businesses of a name brand. That way, you are able to get a constant stream of new followers for your brand.

Also, when writing a description for content, filter your new potential audiences by carefully choosing to which groups does your business actually belong and identify with. For example, if you run a small leather goods shop, you could put #leathergoodies #genuineleather #fashion #ootd #style in a new purse description. Oftentimes, customers will source out a brand using generic categories to allow for a reasonable amount of variety within the premise of what they're looking for- It creates a network where your page falls into, and a certain feel of belonging emerges in customers.

18. Make the content genuine

Facebook based businesses are like sharks in the red ocean. That's the first obstacle most newly made entrepreneurs usually oversee. Kim and Mauborgne's Red Ocean vs. Blue Ocean theory is widely applicable in Facebook marketing, maybe even more than in general management practice.

So what is it all about? To get things straight, it is based on the belief that entrepreneurs should create their own market, rather than starting the game of "hide and seek" with their competition. It is usually really tough if you start to directly face your opponents in a huge red ocean of them. The main goal is to make your own blue ocean! CEO's should make their own competitive benefit by creating valuable content (speaking Facebook marketing wise) which must be genuine, unique, authentic and catchy.

Entrepreneurs (especially old ones) mostly underestimate the power of this kind of marketing. In the theory of marketing, it falls under the category of inbound marketing, which concludes in creating something truly original, which would naturally attract wanted customers to your business and start generating sales! And you guessed right, it's great content! It is really
sad that most people haven't got in touch with all the creative and smart people out there specialized in creating new content.

Why did I emphasize them being creative? They don't necessarily need to be creative art- wise speaking, but those people (maybe you don't even have to outsource them, because they're somewhere around you) have that certain something that's all about knowing the way people think, their psychology, basic visual skills, and a medium level of text content writing. And integrating those things, as the hardest part of it, in my humble opinion.

Focus on two things was in-your-eyes-straight in this content marketing campaign.

- PERSONALIZATION – If there was a double uppercase format, it would be used on this word. I cannot emphasize enough the importance of it. We live in an era where everything is approachable. So what was the easy way to differentiate classic Coke bottles? This was the way. It actually didn't cost much. Everyone wants a product tailored specifically to them. Brands can use that to relate to their customers and stand out. This was the best way to achieve that.

- IMPLEMENTATION – Did I mention the low-cost of this campaign? All the money Coca Cola put into this campaign was used to research its markets and find the most common names and maybe to differentiate the printing on the label machine, but that's insignificant. Integrating this in a great post, gives you a boost in sales.

19. Stick to your brand's character

Follow your competitors on all markets they want to dive in, but avoid having the same image placed to the audience. Remember, your mission and vision is what makes you unique. We're not aiming at making sales by selling more products or services due to low price, we want to gain competitive advantage by selling something which we believe into, and something where so much energy was invested. All those efforts create a specific brand image, lying deeply in every customer's subconscious.

Stick to an attribute that you defined as the most relevant during the process of determining goals, because most of the time limited resources won't allow you to access all the potential ways of spreading through the market. You chose quality?

Outline quality as the most important in your Facebook content. Delivery methods? Emphasize the speed and the importance of time saving nowadays. Simply see what works best for you.

20. Distinguish Facebook from other social media

Every platform of social media is a one of a kind piece in a puzzle, and you should respect that when it comes to doing business online. Different people have different accounts on different social networks, and they do that for various reasons. Sometimes they come for the photos, sometimes it's for the text, and at other times for the latest news. That's what makes Facebook posts unique.

In most cases, they make the best out of both worlds by combining both text and image rich content, which is not the case with Instagram or Twitter. Instagram is all about graphic content with little text in their captions, while Twitter relies on frequent particles of text sometimes combined with images and articles. The versatility of Facebook is the reason I see it as the best platform for all kinds of enterprises and startups, because it's made for everyone.

Nonetheless, realizing and knowing what content goes where isn't the only job. It is possible to post an image on Instagram, text on Twitter (regarding the image) and a Facebook post that somewhat resembles a fusion of the two, but maybe there's a better idea. It is always wise to post different things on different social media platforms. Not only can you alter the posts to appeal to the specific audience on that platform, you can also entice them to follow your pages across all 3 platforms and that something that creates a big connection. Engagement of this kind is something that the marketer has to respect, but in the end, it is created by providing customers with different kinds of content or every individual to indulge in.

21. Marketing as a whole

We mentioned the part with the importance of well educated people who need to specialize in social media marketing. Marketing as a branch needs financing, human resources, management and organization, so implementing your digital strategies in work needs approval from the people from other sectors.

For example, you figure out you made some great posts and all you need is the money for some boosting and sponsored ad management. However, your accountant forbids you from doing that because the budget is currently reserved for improving the product itself. The aftermath here is you carefully choosing other techniques for increasing engagement etc. Also, the "marketing as a whole" concept could refer to complementing Facebook with other digital marketing tools such as Google

Analytics, Pay-Per-Click, Search Engine Optimization, keywords etc. Good communication between social media managers and, for example, SEO experts is a must.

22. Make them know the staff

Now here is an interesting tip. We all know that it is the PR branch of an organization that is responsible for creating posts and keeping in touch with the audience and other community's management. But speaking from the consumer's perspective, it is a fact that's not so rarely forgotten.

Everyone likes a nice and personal touch, but simply sitting in front of our screens and staring at ads removes the humanity from it. As such, it would be nice if every now and then, customers see the people who engage with them daily; this can be achieved by posting a pic from your newest meeting or brainstorming session, or a funny face one of your community managers made.

You could make use of this even further and encourage customer interactions by encouraging them to do the same in the comments!

23. Have good time management skills

Despite this being treated as a segment of business that has less value than other things, I have to mention a few things. First, keeping up a good page with great content isn't easy at all. Many entrepreneurs underestimate the level of difficulty involved, and tend to neglect it.

It is really important for entrepreneurs to realize that and start leaving enough time for this. Sure, everyone wants to see an outcome of rapid boosting sales through the aid of Facebook, but doesn't want to dedicate time to content creation and interacting with people. This will result in unsustainable profits, simply a temporary boom for the business.

24. Try new things

Of course, conformism is great and cozy and warm. Repeated business practices make great patterns which have always turned out great, evident from the fact that they have been around for decades. But the world is constantly changing, especially in the area of social media marketing. Something that provided good results yesterday doesn't mean it will be the same today. Constant research and improvement is a must, just like in any other area of business.

Besides generating new sales with new methods of marketing, customers always love to see something new and fresh being posted. Despite the marketer's effort to make his or her content special, if he constantly reuses old methods, customers would feel bored. So step outside the comfort zone, and test out one of those new methods you've been longing to try!

25. Integration

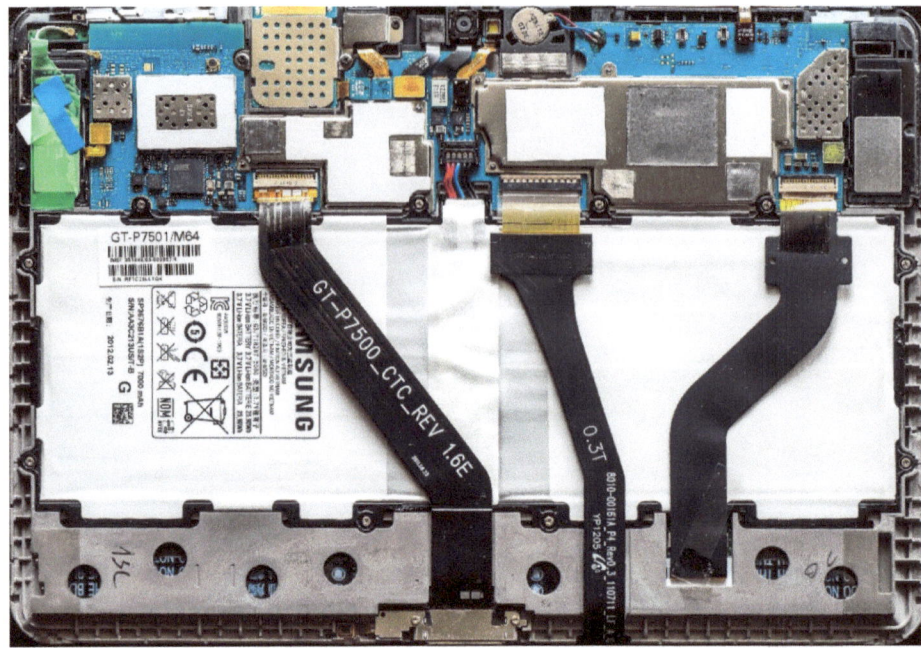

The whole point of this guide wasn't for you to choose one strategy and stick to it till the end. These strategies work in synergy, and their success lies in being able to incorporate them seamlessly into your practice.

Many businesses specialize in some marketing practices, while being newbies in other fields of marketing. The best marketers out there are able to master all of these, and do well in implementing all of them in their business. This is the true art of advertising. Of course, some strategies may come across as contradictory at times, but every single one of them has perks that others don't have, and vice versa.

Within a marketing team, employees may have varying degrees of experience and knowledge on marketing, and graphic designers, community managers and post managers need to work together to utilise their strengths and weaknesses in the best way possible. Qualities such as logical thinking, good communication, and adaptability are also useful in other areas in life, not just in Facebook marketing.

www.ingramcontent.com/pod-product-compliance
Lightning Source LLC
Chambersburg PA
CBHW051820210526
45473CB00005B/1676